Birthright

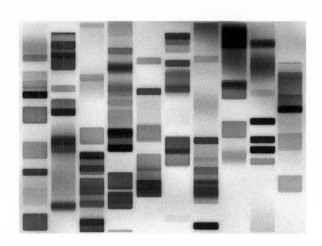

RACHEL GIPPETTI

Birthright

EYEWEAR AVIATOR

2016 SERIES

First published in 2016
by Eyewear Publishing Ltd
Suite 333, 19-21 Crawford Street
Marylebone, London W1H 1PJ
United Kingdom

Typeset with graphic design by Edwin Smet
Author photograph by Angélique Kergosien
Printed in England by Lightning Source

ISBN 978-1-911335-11-5

Eyewear wishes to thank Jonathan Wonham for his generous patronage of our press.

WWW.EYEWEARPUBLISHING.COM

4

For my mother

TABLE OF CONTENTS

AVIATOR

THE UNFORTUNATE BODY

When Eli and Alejandro squared up outside the gym
I was clinging to the chain-link fence on the far side of the field.
Alejandro's face was egg white and when his fist jumped
like a snake into Eli's cheek I heard a sound like steak
falling on kitchen tiles.

When watching boxers punch each other
I am amazed that their faces stay on their bones.
Shocked that their deltoids do not slough off
like corners of slow cooked pork.

There can be space
where there was body, but your arms
cannot climb the fence without you. Your brain stays
in its case, but desperate, changes
into a plump red glove.

SPECIFIC INHERITED MUTATIONS

'A typo occurs every 100,000 nucleotides', which means

100,000 female swordfish swam like a shadow, under the belly of a cargo boat
containing flat-packed X-ray machines, then stabbed the boat,
      which cracked and sank,
the radioactive waves crashing to the seabed, where I slept
on our honeymoon in Greece, typing, blissful in my sleep.

Or the nucleus of a dream I had (where we made love in my parent's bed)
      was damaged
when I woke up suddenly.
10am at work, while typing, I developed an allergy to Tide Ultra, so
while scratching my thigh, things got typoed.

Or a bilateral tide at Jones Beach on Long Island tore off my bikini top,
which was sucked into a glass bottle, then washed onto Beach Park shoreline,
where a young girl, with a long red braid, found it
and wrote back to me. An amateur writer,
her letter contained numerous typos.

Or my mother wrote a poem, in which she encoded a secret,
adding 100,000 letters to the alphabet. She buried
the poem in a red maple box, at the bottom of the Muddy River. Over the years

the tides tugged the box through the silt, into the Atlantic. I don't understand
the process of water filtration, but this morning, when I turned on the tap
the box popped out into the womb of my teapot
and while drinking my tea, I got it.

KEEPING IT TO MYSELF

Some words should stay unsettled
breath, fidgeting behind the teeth.

Some words make you a prophet,
eyes white in a lightning storm.

Holy being without control
of your mind. I keep the words

under my tongue. Let them dissolve
like a sour pill.

I'd call, but Boston's sleeping
and maybe in your dream

you have supernatural powers.
Maybe you pull squalling babes from

the cold remains of bonfires, or swim
through molten Mount Vesuvius.

You might know what the gulls are laughing at,
might warm leftovers

just by loving them.
I'm merely an anxious mortal

with no intention
of interrupting your dream.

ANOTHER SECRET FAMILY RECIPE

Inside the room of fine china
there's a smell of pickled onion.
Flour the paper walls. Toss the greens

in the clear glass. My hands
are wooden up to the elbow,
fingers stiff and slick with oil.

The glasses keep breaking.
The crystal rain falls into the deep
ceramic sea. The whole room

smells of seahorses,
of whales, of starfish.
Or is it just salmon again?

I'll peel the scales off the sizzling pan
and throw them back
into the foam.

You are some of the few
who know my ancestry. I shed
my fins, my gills sealed

as smiling scars. Only you
around this table know of my scales,
my lust for salt and excessive thirst.

See my shins, my secret
lineage. Blood lines of Omega3.
The threads of white bone,

followed by green leaves,
peeled roots and oil.

HOME VIDEO JOKESTER

With scissors I cut stars into the asphalt.
Their crooked flash illuminates my faith
in Marie Kondo and medical school, in atoms and antibiotics.

Roll the moment when I look down Chester Ave in the dark,
ankles aching in my rollerblades. Under the streetlights
out step solemn squirrels, possums, street dogs, to cut me down,
one weak ankle at a time.

I push the wheels forward, pick up speed on the slope,
while the cameraman quips, 'It's all uphill from here'.

TAKEAWAY

The smart ass fortune cookie
tells me to trust my intuition.

I digest the fortune cookie.
Is eating food that mimics fabric wise?

I fold my handkerchiefs
and swallow them whole.

It's newly proven
to be life threatening.

Epicurus makes the best
wonton soup this side of Devon.

One of the hardest things
about moving to Devon. The lack

of ethnic restaurants was a void.
I give the skin of a roast potato its due.

I give them an hour in the oven,
cut the roof of my mouth open on them.

But make that a blister, fiery and full
bulging at the bully nudge of my tongue

burned to life on boiling broth
and crumbled pork, that hid sweating

sesame oil inside a delicate noodle
gently folded like a tiny hanky

then, instantly I know what to do
and remember how to chew.

TEETH

If I still lived in America maybe
I would not be having these bad dreams
about my teeth – I wake
grinding in the half-light.

When there is not enough light
anything can happen. When I was seventeen
I found a hand in my waistband (it wasn't
my hand). Someone took
my handbag home by accident.
The next morning they put their hand
inside. Everything felt cluttered
and strange. The sensation
was incapable of memory. There is probably

life out there.
There are billions of fizzing stars. There are
planets just like ours. Planets made of rose
quartz and cold. If a meteor hit,
they would explode
like a heavy crystal serving bowl.

*Outer space is not a void. Things in the dark
have colour.* Like white is not white,
my teeth, the colour
of bedside table lamplight.

MORNING MEDITATION

I'm lying on my back again.
My morning ritual helps me

forget the context of things.
I'd like to recontextualise

the reasons that I sweat at night.
If religious I could

find meaning in the smell of toast burning.
I have disappointed my mother.

Have I disappointed my mother?
If I could have another Batmitzva

I would read a different passage
and definitely wear a different dress.

Something tight that more accurately reflects
my unreligious personality.

The clouds are soft and comforting.
They pat my face with a cool washcloth

and they play with my hair.
It's important to wake up early

and get your bearings
because if you are tired and confused

and try to introduce a new song to the world
or make toast from frozen bread,

feeding it into the toaster again and again,
well, you know what will happen.

GONE WILD

The curiosity of mastectomy
Muscle folded over the silicone
Foetal cow tissue, pectoral stitches
Pushed up, out, ouch

O if only you could see me now
Drawn in my wet white T-shirt, wild
In my pale green hospital gown, wild
Synthetic sunflowers on the windowsill
Wild white spirits, cold
Like snow balls, puff
Puff of pale skin

O if only you could see me then
Softer than suede, sagging
Like snowdrops, knowing
Like an owl that everything is fragments
Fur and bone and wild
With vertigo
The ascending mouse
Who gasps
O O

ALARM VS. ATARAXIA

We balance the clock on a stack of books.
Your arms make grand gestures
but barely move.

The alarm goes off at three minute intervals.

I dream of the leak above the stove.
We still don't know
where the water is coming from.

The alarm goes off.
The ceiling collapses.
The water rushes.

I repeat this every three minutes
and in between demand that you hold me.

For long moments
I swim in a still pond,
where water is supposed to be.

BIRTHRIGHT

My Birthright trip to Israel expired.
In pictures on the website
Israel looks bright and dry.

Deep Red Sea.
Remember the plagues?
Body of water becomes

body of blood. Body of blood
becomes test tube of BRCA2.
God becomes a Google-search
if God chooses.

Cruelty to animals was the theme
of my Torah reading. I disapprove
of sacrifice, devour grass fed
fillet steak. Epicurus, is it too late

to lace my veins with milk?
It's turned my milk to blood,
my God to Epicurus,
turned the clocks forward

like an urge. My friends are holding
their firstborns close, and I hold mine
so deep inside that
I needn't worry. But I do

take care to check the dates
and sniff the jars. Some smell
sour and some smell sweet
as I imagine Israel might smell

AVIATOR

like grandmother's skirt, a puddle
of goat's blood in the grass,
mother's milk, morning wine,
an ice cream melting in a red sea,

a salty puddle, a sprig of green,
an egg, a bone, a crisp,
a bite, a kiss, it's past
expiry.

ANIMAL POEM

I am very concerned about the smog.
I am also concerned that the birds and squirrels will turn to stone.

Headaches could potentially be the end. I learned
that from Caroline, the gold fish,

her short shimmering tail.
Who else has imagined their shadow as a shark

beneath them in the deep end of the pool?
I always imagine the best possible

outcome because otherwise
I have panic attacks.

Panic attacks are like bear hugs
from real bears.

THE SACRIFICE MEETS THE KONMARI METHOD [1]

I light a fire. Begin
with my clothes. Empty, they keep me

vain, but warm. My temperature runs cold so stick close
when the woollens go up.

I burn books, sparing tomes with thrills
of joy. Just to hold.

Leaf-pile pages, I jog
to the Esso for matches. It's not destruction

it's domestic, an actual Method.
Yanking paperwork from drawers, I feel no joy at all.

You pace loudly. I tell you to take off your shoes
then burn them. I'm sorry

it took me so long to discover these strategies.
Tidying was not my thing, like the copper coil

was not my thing. Like eating jellied meat
was revolting. Though now

I'll eat pork pies. If it wasn't for your doctorate
we might not know Tarkovsky, might not

have to burn it all twice. Ashamed
to be naked now. My bra is smoke choking

---

1 A method of de-cluttering, which can be found in the guide, *The Life Changing Magic of Tidying Up* by
Marie Kondo. The method involves discarding belonging that don't bring you joy when you touch them.

the lungs of a seagull. Listen to its racket
feel no joy at this either.

There's no catching the gull, to throw on the pyre.
I tried. Though I'm sure

there's a Method. And look
our house has never been tidier.

DRESSY

Black sequined dress
you're garbage.
No. You're not
mine anymore. You're
bin-bag trashy. I was
always polite to
strangers who
groped my classy
mind, I never
discovered sweaty
public houses until
I discovered my
husband puking
freshman year. Ah
nostalgia you're
not my belonging
any longer. I'd be
puking first
trimester. No
feeling bad
about multiple
follicles all the time.
A night out, a clear
out would do
wonders for hormone
levels. What
should I wear?
I lost my sparkly
to a charity shop
deposit point. I gave
it all away

to strangers.
I gave blow
dries to Shannon,
Tara, Sarah. On
prom night we
glued diamantes
to our eyelids.

'THE UNIVERSE IS AN ORANGE'

my father explained, followed by
something about textured skin, the segments
were vital like atoms.
SunnyD in slices, the juice
of life. I think
a thumbnail nicked the universe. Its scent
was there when I walked in the room.
His girlfriend dreamt:
That segments divided inside me.
I explained that the child
only grew in my heart.
My father explained:
I turned his pinky finger into his heart
when I gripped it in my walnut fist.
My father explained Alan Guth's theory
of cosmic inflation. My father always knew
that the universe was round
and inflates: An orange,
a walnut, a vitamin C supplement,
a heart inside a walnut,
an orange growing inside a heart.

BLUE KIMONO

I leave 32 bursting bin-liners in front of St Luke's Hospice Shop.
If you forgot, I said that I would face my deepest fears.
After I watched the YouTube video of a huntsman spider
trapped in a banana bag, angry and afraid, I went
to the charity shop. I looked carefully for something
that belonged to my mother. She never gave me
permission to wear her blue kimono, but I wore it
until I was thirty-two. She told me not to
be scared, so of course, I feel less
terrified since I stuffed the blue kimono
into a black bin-liner.

When I decided to stop
wearing dead women's clothes, I felt...
Epicurus, tell me how to feel
like this is my new vice. I try to birth
a new plucky me with each new moon
rather than make a mess
with all that red moon, yellow moon
type of experience. That kind
of dreamy, milk moon, movie kind
of experience, like *One Born Every Minute*.

Wait (I decide to wait)
                    I go back

to the black moon,
where my mother and Epicurus
slowly dance, where there's no light.
I can't see her face in front of my hand.
My hand feels like a huntsman spider

AVIATOR

but I hold it there
skittering in the dark, and stare cross-eyed
into the crater.

THE GARDEN

I forget who pulled the rose stems
from the rib holes, each barbed
helix coiled deep.

Red petals lipped a foil pot.
You never dropped one (whoever you are)
you're gifted, a green thumb.

Every part of the skin survived
and thrived, despite the spade
the rake, the pick, the roots.

I miss views over the wet fields
of Hayle. Not a bed of straw
or the product of funding cuts

but the Garden, with pink walls
and grounds the colour of
artichoke, mantis, moss.

After April rain I don't grow back
but season after season
I'm evergreen.

IN THE MIDDLE OF THE ENCORE

I fainted in the pit of an Iggy Pop and the Stooges concert.
Woke up on the gummy floor outside the men's room
knowing death was nothing to us.

If you're alone and you got the fear
I disappeared before
I felt floor.

Happiness is a guarantee – Of course
I can't confirm anything, though now I know
the edges of things are anthems.

On stage, Iggy's jeans slung low, we could see
our ancestry.

          Whatever I saw between

crushed beer cans, black boots
and your flurried face over me,
was standing in a quiet fog.

It was made for you and me.
We live on the lip of a mug.

Let's not wait
until the spin of morning
to wake up.

I'M GRATEFUL I HATE THIS

since I can't drink I pour
then spluttering try
to bail the broken boat
oops Epricurus
pleasure me already
but Epicurus won't
be pressured into things
like me and my big
interest in portals
which are definitely
not problems opening
onto worlds of water
full of people whispering
litanies blinkity blinkity
blink blink blink all night long
and not one wink
nausea is a symptom
of what's happening
to my breath in time
with the wind picking up
where two seas meet in Prasonisi
they kiss at high tide
while we're finally kissing
I count this as drinking
and I'm pissed
that I don't feel old enough
to be doing this
blood test I'll pass it
on to my daughter I'll tell her
it's watermelon flavoured
we'll learn how to swallow it

together we won't fear
human fluids seeping
in the guest room that smells
of lavender oil glugging
water that tastes of paper
I'm grateful and pour the full moon
over my head SPLASH
I hang upside down
while you rub my back
SMACK I'm reminded
some feel lucky
on a leaking raft

UNIFORMS

We live next to a high school for girls.
Walking to school in chittering clumps

they seem happy enough, but I don't know
if I agree with uniforms. If we follow

nature, animals are naked. Spiders' eyes are not
tiny black buttons. I've forgotten

the nature of high school. Hungry spiders
with desires and anxiety.

*

There is a box of buttons in the drawer
of my bedside table. One day I sew the buttons

onto a uniform for my baby.
An unpredictable uniform

made of leaves. My baby
blends with the park across the street.

When my baby walks to school
the neighbours think:

Look at that beautiful swirl of leaves in the wind.

ACKNOWLEDGEMENTS

Thank you to Todd Swift for giving me the opportunity to share my work. Many thanks, to Anthony Caleshu for his long-standing encouragement and consistently good advice. I have deep gratitude for my husband, Allister Gall, for his support of my poetry and for helping me take my hands off the controls. Above all, thank you to my parents; my father Louis Gippetti, who, delightfully, makes sense of life in metaphor, and whose love and support is always palpable despite the distance. Eternal thanks to my mother, Laura May Schulman, who knew, that through poetry, there would never be silence between us.

'Another Secret Family Recipe', previously published in *Shearsman* Magazine.

'Alarm vs. Ataraxia', previously published in *The Stinging Fly*.